NOTORIOUS AMERICANS AND THEIR TIMES

Belle STAR R
and the Wild West

by

CORINNE J. NADEN AND ROSE BLUE

BLACKBIRCH PRESS, INC.

WOODBRIDGE, CONNECTICUT

Published by Blackbirch Press, Inc.
260 Amity Road
Woodbridge, CT 06525

e-mail: staff@blackbirch.com
Web site: www.blackbirch.com

©2000 by Blackbirch Press, Inc.
First Edition

Printed in China

10 9 8 7 6 5 4 3 2 1

Library of Congress Cataloging-in-Publication Data
Naden, Corinne J.
Belle Starr and the Wild West / Corinne J. Naden and Rose Blue.
     p.   cm. — (Notorious Americans and their times)
     Includes index.
     Summary: A biography of the legendary outlaw known as the Bandit Queen. Sidebars describe the history, daily life, and people of the Wild West.
     ISBN 1-56711-223-4 (alk. paper)
     1. Starr, Belle, 1848–1889—Juvenile literature. 2. Women out-laws—West (U.S.)—Biography—Juvenile literature. 3. Outlaws—West (U.S.)—Biography—Juvenile literature. 4. West (U.S.)—Biography—Juvenile literature. 5. Frontier and pioneer life—West (U.S.)—Juvenile literature. [1.Starr, Belle, 1848-1889. 2. Robbers and out-laws. 3. Women—Biography. 4. West (U.S.)—History. 5. Frontier and pioneer life—West (U.S.)] I. Blue, Rose. II. Title. III. Series.
F594.S8 N34   2000
364.15'5'092—dc21   00-008437
                                                                            CIP
                                                                            AC

Table of Contents

A FIGHT IN THE STREET.

Chapter 1

A WAR BEGINS
A STARR RISES

$\mathcal{I}$f you believe the tales of the Old West, or the Wild West as it was often called, the western landscape was populated with stereotypes. Every gunslinger had nerves of steel and a heart of stone. Every saloon had a dancer with the face of an angel and a heart of gold. And every quick-on-the-draw sheriff always got his outlaw. The tales of the Wild West weren't the way it really happened, but the stories had just enough truth in them to keep them alive through the decades.

Opposite: Common legends of the Old West include gunslingers, saloons, and shoot-outs in the streets.

The tales of the West spoke of larger-than-life characters with fanciful names like "Six-Toed" Pete or "Turkey Creek" Jack Johnson. They included "Wild Bill" Hickock and Jesse James, Bat Masterson and Billy the Kid, Wyatt Earp and Doc Holliday, and the Younger brothers. These Wild West lawmen, bandits, and killers shot it out in places like Deadwood, Dodge City, and Tombstone. The shoot-outs occurred inside the Long Branch Saloon and outside the O.K. Corral. Ladies were part of the Wild West scene, too. There was Calamity Jane, Annie Oakley, and Belle Starr—the Bandit Queen.

Who Was Belle Starr?

Why was Belle Starr called the Bandit Queen? Was she really an outlaw? Some people say Belle was "plain as mud" and a tender, devoted mother in a checkered apron. Others insist that Belle was a "beauty in velvet" who wore pistols around her waist as she rode horseback across the countryside. Exactly what is the real story of Belle Starr?

The fact is that no one knows for sure. Whatever was true about Belle Starr—and many famous figures of the Old West—was so altered by newspaper

Some of the Old West's lawmen became legends in their own right. Wyatt Earp (third from left) and Bat Masterson (second from right) are two of the most famous.

reporters and story writers of the time that most of the truth got lost in legend. People back East hungered for tales of gunslinging outlaws and bar-room shoot-outs. The press recognized that hunger

DIME NOVELS

"Dime novels" of the late 1800s had catchy titles and subtitles: *Buffalo Bills' Strategy* or *The Queen of Crater Cave*; *Wild Bill, The Wild West Duelist* or *The Girl Mascot of Moonlight Mine*; and *Deadwood Dick on Deck* or *Calamity Jane, The Heroine of Whoop-Up*. They were widely read and sold from 1860 until 1910, but they weren't really novels as much as they were tall tales about a real person who had exaggerated abilities. The selling price of most "dime novels" was actually closer to a nickel than a dime. And for that, the reader got adventure, romance, and a taste for the Wild West.

Here's a description of Calamity Jane from an early novel. "Now she dashed away through the narrow gulch, catching with delight long breaths of the perfume of flowers which met her nostrils at every

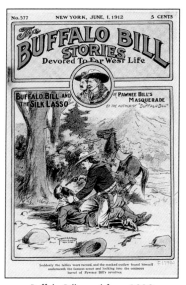

Buffalo Bill novel from 1912.

onward leap of her horse, piercing the gloom of the night with her dark lovely eyes, searchingly, lest she should be surprised; lighting a cigar at full motion...."

The dime novel industry was started by Erastus Beadle, a printer from Albany, New York, who learned his trade by printing labels on flour sacks. After he had established himself in New York City with a network of both writers and printers, he set up the publishing firm of Beadle and Adams. Altogether the company published over 2,000 titles. The plots involved huge casts of characters who accomplished impossible tasks and had improbable adventures—all in a Western setting. Out of these cheap novels came many of the stereotypes of gunslingers and outlaws who had populated the Wild West. One of these characters was Belle Starr.

and "adjusted" the stories for their readers back home. It didn't matter if the tales were true or not. What mattered was creating daring stories about the Wild West that Eastern readers could imagine without having to experience it firsthand.

Life Shrouded in Mystery

The debate about what is fact or fiction in Belle Shirley Starr's life begins with her birthdate. Some historians claim that the date on her tombstone is wrong. They base their conclusions on how old she was for other events in her life and on early records. Belle's actual birthdate may have been as early as 1846 or as late as 1856. The birthdate on her tombstone, however, says February 5, 1848.

The United States census of the Shirley family taken in 1850 also lists Belle's age as 2, which would make 1848 the correct year of her birth.

Early Years in Carthage

Belle was born into what was, for the time, a somewhat prosperous and proper family. She was most likely born on a farm about 12 miles from the town of Carthage, Missouri. Her father was John Shirley, a

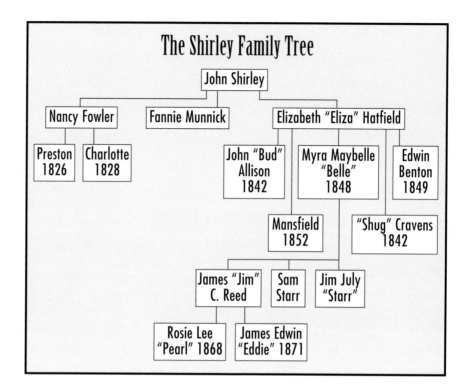

The Shirley Family Tree

John Shirley

- Nancy Fowler
  - Preston 1826
  - Charlotte 1828
- Fannie Munnick
- Elizabeth "Eliza" Hatfield
  - John "Bud" Allison 1842
  - Myra Maybelle "Belle" 1848
    - Mansfield 1852
    - "Shug" Cravens 1842
    - James "Jim" C. Reed
      - Rosie Lee "Pearl" 1868
      - James Edwin "Eddie" 1871
    - Sam Starr
    - Jim July "Starr"
  - Edwin Benton 1849

native of Virginia who had moved to Kentucky with his family. As a young man, John Shirley had moved to Indiana to raise horses. He married Nancy Fowler and had two children, Preston and Charlotte. That marriage, as well as a second one to Fannie Munnick, ended in divorce. The third marriage was the charm for John, however. He married teenaged Eliza Hatfield and moved to Jasper County in southwestern Missouri.

White settlers had been moving into this area in Missouri after members of the Osage tribe of Native

Americans had been driven off their hunting grounds. It was an area in the Ozark Mountains, full of sparkling streams, fertile land, and abundant wildlife. John Shirley bought about 800 acres of farmland near a small settlement, later called Georgia City, on the North Fork of Spring River. He was a good businessman and a successful farmer, raising crops, hogs, and horses. By the standards of the time, the Shirleys lived well.

John and Liza eventually had five children. The second of the five—and their only daughter—was named Myra Maybelle. The family called her May, although she later began calling herself Bella, or Belle. Her four brothers were John Allison, Edwin Benton, Mansfield, and Cravens. In 1856, when Belle was eight years old, the family moved to Carthage, a town of less than 500 residents and the Jasper County seat. With the money from the sale of his farm, John Shirley built the Carthage Hotel, an inn and tavern that included a stable and blacksmith shop. The local newspaper advertised: "Carthage Hotel, North Side Public Square, John Shirley, Proprietor, Horses and Hacks for Hire, A good stable attached."

In addition to his business sense, John Shirley was admired for his fine library, which contained novels, biographies, and books on philosophy. The fact that he had any books at all put him in a class well above the average citizen. John Shirley loved to tell of his southern political leanings, while others gathered around and listened. He was so well respected in Jasper county that he was called "Judge" Shirley.

"Judge" Shirley was often consulted on matters of importance to the town, including a charter for the Carthage Female Academy in 1855. It is not surprising, therefore, that Belle attended the academy. All the best families of Carthage sent their daughters there.

A Not-So-Proper Southern Lady

As a young girl, Belle was once described by the local Carthage Press as "dark-haired and intelligent." At the academy, she studied grammar, arithmetic, spelling, reading, Latin, Greek, and music. Prompted by her mother, Belle also learned to be a "proper Southern lady." Mrs. Shirley especially loved to have Belle play the piano for hotel guests. Myra Belle may not have been a brilliant pianist, but she did have a captive audience.

Myra's mother may have been pleased with her daughter's musical talent, but young Myra Belle had other interests. She loved roaming the Ozark hills on horseback with her older brother John Allison, better known by the family nickname, "Bud." The future Belle Starr also had a sharp temper and was ready to use her fists on anyone who crossed her. From Bud, Belle learned not only to ride horses but also to handle a gun. Underneath the proper Southern lady was a spoiled little girl who mostly got what she wanted.

But the comfortable world of twelve-year-old Belle Shirley was about to change drastically. In December 1860, divisions between North and South—mostly on the issue of slavery and states' rights—were reaching a crisis stage. South Carolina seceded (withdrew) from the United States of America, followed by its neighbors Mississippi, Florida, Alabama, Louisiana, Georgia, and Texas. These states were later joined by Arkansas, North Carolina, Tennessee, and Virginia. Together they formed a new union, which they called the Confederate States of America. On April 12, 1861, South Carolina fired on Fort Sumter, a federal outpost in the harbor of Charleston. The nation was officially at war.

A State Divided

The state of Missouri was not sure which side to join. Should it stay with the Union (North) or join the Confederacy (South)? Missouri had joined the Union under the Missouri Compromise of 1820. At that time, the United States was a union of eleven free and eleven slave states. Missouri had applied for statehood as a slave state, and Maine had applied as a free state. The Missouri Compromise that brought these states into the Union admitted one slave state and one free state, but it banned slavery from the Louisiana Territory north of Missouri's southern border, except for Missouri. People realized this compromise would eventually lead to more free states than slave states.

During the years leading up to the Civil War, a movement against slavery had gained support in Missouri. Violent fights erupted between Missourians who were for slavery and those who were against it. The Kansas-Nebraska Act of 1854 only made matters worse. With this act, the Nebraska territory was divided into two states, Nebraska and Kansas. Kansas was so upset by the division that it became a vicious battle-ground for pro- and anti-slavery activists. Because of

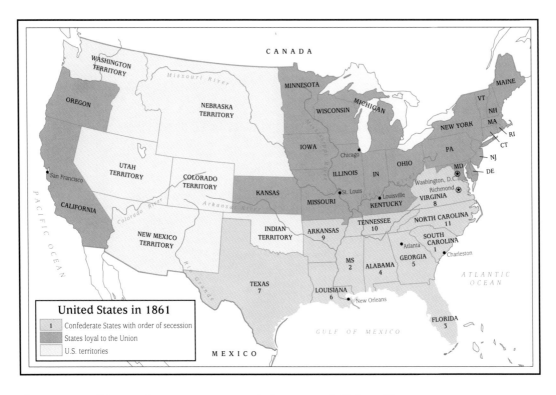

United States in 1861
1	Confederate States with order of secession
	States loyal to the Union
	U.S. territories

these conflicts, the state was nicknamed "bleeding Kansas." The small war between Kansas and Nebraska spilled over into the lands that bordered the area. Many people in Missouri developed a hatred for these violent neighbors on their western border.

By 1861, the whole country was at war. Even though Missouri was a slave state, its people still had to decide which side they would join. The Missouri governor, Claiborne F. Jackson, was personally for slavery, but he thought it best for Missouri to stay in

Missouri was at the center of the slavery issue in 1861. The state ultimately decided to remain in the Union and abolish slavery.

the Union. The state legislature agreed. About a quarter of Missouri's sons didn't agree. They wanted to fight on the side of the Confederacy. The state remained divided—a hotbed of conflict and turmoil—during the Civil War.

Jefferson Davis was President of the Confederate States of America during the Civil War.

A War Begins: A Starr Rises

The Battle at Coon Creek

Within the Shirley family, father John was described as a "hot-blooded southerner." He cheered when Fort Sumter was attacked. He cheered louder when the first battle of the war ended in a southern victory at Bull Run in Manassas, Virginia, on July 21, 1861. His pro-slavery enthusiasm filtered down to the Shirley children. And if their father's southern sympathies didn't sway them, the fight at Coon Creek near Carthage most likely did.

After Fort Sumter in Charleston Harbor fell, President Abraham Lincoln called for Missouri to send its quota (fair share) of volunteers for the Union army. Governor Jackson refused. Instead, the governor called for men to defend the state against the Union. A Confederate flag was raised in Sarcoxie, a town in Jasper County. On July 4, 1861, Union and Confederate troops met at Coon

Fort Sumter, in Charleston, South Carolina, was the site of the first battle of the Civil War.

Creek near Carthage. The battle lasted all day and reached the outskirts of town. In the end, the Confederate troops withdrew, and Carthage was occupied by a small group of Union soldiers. John Shirley and other Confederate sympathizers were furious.

Bushwacker "Bud"

Jasper County became the site of bitter fighting throughout the war. The outcome of the Coon Creek battle and the constant fighting inspired eighteen-year-old Bud Shirley to get involved. He joined a band of bushwhackers, a name given to guerrilla fighters who stirred up unrest. Their goal was to make the Union keep large numbers of troops in Missouri to stay and fight against them. That way the Union troops couldn't be sent to fight at more important battlefronts in the South. Belle watched with pride as Bud rode off to join them. For her part, she vowed to do whatever she could to make life unpleasant for the Yankees (northerners).

And make trouble she did. According to one tale, in 1862, Belle went on a scouting mission for her brother. Belle was returning home after spying on

Union troops when she was stopped by Major Edwin B. Eno (or Enos) of the U.S. Army. Major Eno had heard that Bud was at home in Carthage, and he was determined to capture Bud. When the major stopped Belle, he was sure she was on her way to warn her brother about his possible capture. Eno held the young girl under arrest to give his own men enough time to reach Carthage and capture Belle's brother. Then he let Belle go, saying, "My men will have your brother under arrest before you reach him."

Soldiers, who were injured in battle, were brought to field hospitals like this one.

However, the major underestimated the young girl. She rode the backroads to Carthage with such speed that when Eno's troops entered the town, she was already there waiting for them. Politely, she informed the startled soldiers that Captain Bud Shirley had left town about "half an hour ago."

According to another story, a year later Major Eno was a guest at the home of the Richey family one evening. They lived in Newtonia, about 35 miles from Carthage. When Belle stopped that particular evening, she told the Richeys she had lost her way. She asked if she could stay overnight. The Richeys were pro-Union people, and Belle was actually hoping to overhear information she could pass on to her Confederate friends. Belle played the piano after supper and overheard someone say that Eno's troops were using the Richey's stone barn as their barracks. The next morning after she left the Richey's, Belle managed to tell her Confederate friends. Soon after, a fire destroyed the Richey's barn.

One lingering rumor claims that Belle was part of William C. Quantrill's raiders and that she rode with him dressed as a man. Most historians doubt that she ever even met Quantrill. However, Belle's boyfriend

Abraham Lincoln, shown here in an early photo, became president in 1861, just as the Civil War was beginning.

at the time, James C. Reed, did join Quantrill's men at the age of seventeen.

In the first years of the Civil War, Confederate troops won many victories, often against much larger Union forces. Then, Confederate General Robert E. Lee and his 76,000-man army suffered a major defeat at the Battle of Gettysburg, Pennsylvania, in July 1863. Although the war continued for nearly two more years, Gettysburg was the beginning of the end for the Confederacy. But that didn't matter to the Missouri rebels. They kept up their guerrilla warfare. By 1864, Bud Shirley was one of the most wanted bushwhackers in the state. Union troops got word that Bud and a companion had stopped for supper at a home in the town of Sarcoxie. They surrounded the house. When Shirley tried to flee over a fence, the Union soldiers shot and killed him.

Belle Starr supposedly accompanied her father to Sarcoxie to get Bud's body. With many curious citizens and Union soldiers looking on, John Shirley carried his dead son to the wagon and placed Bud's gun and belt in the wagon beside him. The story goes that when her father went to the barn for Bud's horse, Belle suddenly grabbed the gun and began

~ Quantrill and His Raiders ~

William Clarke Quantrill and his gang of Confederate fighters were guerrillas (independent fighters). They would sweep into a town, rob and kill people, and set buildings on fire. Union sympathizers hated Quantrill.

Born in Ohio in 1837, Quantrill became a schoolteacher. He moved to Kansas and then Utah, where he took

William Clarke Quantrill

up gambling. Quantrill went back to Kansas before the start of the Civil War. He made his living by stealing horses, and he was even charged with murder. When the Civil War began, he joined the Confederates in Missouri for a short time. Then he formed his own band of guerrilla fighters. They became known for their ruthless raids on pro-Union towns and farms in Missouri and Kansas. Just the mere rumor that this band was seen in the area was enough to strike terror into the townspeople. Quantrill and his gang could sweep into a town almost without warning, burn and loot every house, shoot anyone in sight, and be gone within a few hours.

The Quantrill raiders became widely known for their brutal massacre at the free-state stronghold of Lawrence, Kansas, on August 21, 1863. Although they fired on no women, they shot every man or boy they saw. At least 150 were killed. One eyewitness, Julia Lovejoy, describes what happened: "I could see every house this side of Lawrence, with a dense smoke arising from them as they advanced, firing at every house in their march of death."

Toward the end of the war, Quantrill and his bushwackers entered Kentucky disguised as Union soldiers. The trickery worked, and they reveled in brutality. The Union called Quantrill an outlaw, but the Confederacy made him a captain. He was mortally wounded on a raid in Kentucky in 1865.

The battle on Little Round Top in Gettysburg, Pennsylvania, was a key Union victory during the Civil War.

shooting. The citizens were terrified, but the soldiers only laughed. They had taken out all of the remaining bullets from Bud's gun. With Belle in tears and the soldiers laughing, the Shirley family went home.

Other accounts say that Belle accompanied her mother to claim her brother's body. Supposedly, Belle vowed to marry the person who hunted down her brother's killer. It is said that this is the reason that Belle married Jim Reed, her first husband.

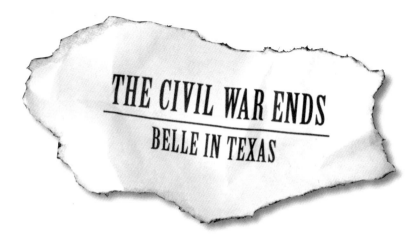

Chapter 2

THE CIVIL WAR ENDS
BELLE IN TEXAS

$\mathscr{B}$ud's death was a terrible blow to John Shirley. He had become beaten down by the war. He was tired of the burning, looting, and killing it had brought to Carthage. He knew it was only a matter of time before his hotel would be destroyed, too. During the summer of 1864, John Shirley sold his property and loaded the family goods into two Conestoga covered wagons. John Shirley took his family to Texas. Some accounts say the family settled briefly in Grapevine, Texas. In 1867, the family ended up in

Scyene, Texas, a small community near Dallas where Preston, his son from his first marriage, lived.

Belle was sixteen years old when the family arrived in Texas during the summer of 1864. Texas had become a state in 1845, and it had joined the Confederacy in 1861.

Wagon trains were the most popular means of transportation for America's many fortune seekers.

John Shirley had picked a wild place to resettle his family. A history of war with Mexico and independence as a republic, together with a lot of land in which to roam, had given a state full of sturdy Texans a reckless daring. The state had become such a safe haven for bandits that the phrase "Gone to Texas," or just "GTT," scrawled on a cabin door was a sign that someone was one step ahead of the law.

On their way to Scyene, the Shirleys passed through Dallas. It had only about 2,000 residents, but the lineup of saloons, eateries, gambling halls, and dance palaces was quickly making it the entertainment center of the Southwest. Never mind that when it rained, the streets were ankle deep in water, or that if you had angry words with a stranger, you could land in the local cemetery!

The Shirleys settled in South Mesquite Creek near Scyene. John Shirley bought farmland and built a four-room house, which was considered rather fancy for the time. Belle went to a one-room school in the area. Her attendance record, however, was spotty. Since Belle had attended a private academy in Missouri, she thought her classmates in Texas were dreary and not worth her attention.

President Lincoln delivered a famous address at Gettysburg at the end of the Civil War.

"Go West, Young Man"

Belle and her family had been among the trickle of Americans heading West before the war ended. Less than a year after the Shirleys arrived in Texas, Confederate forces under General Robert E. Lee surrendered to Union General Ulysses S. Grant at Appomattox Court House, Virginia, on April 9, 1865. The Civil War was officially over. After the Civil War, the trickle of people heading west became a steady stream. People in both the North and South went West to find land and new opportunities. Many were urged on by famed newspaper writer Horace Greeley, who in the 1850s declared, "Go West, young man, and grow up with the country."

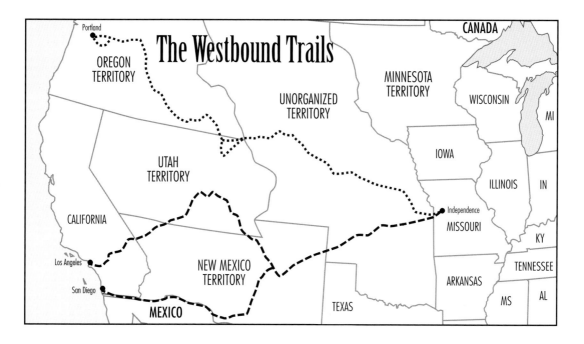

Families moving west stuffed all of their belongings into their wagons. Some wagons could hold up to six tons of goods.

It was one thing to talk about going West, but it was quite another to get there. Railroads didn't connect the eastern and western United States until 1869. The only available choices before that were wagons, stagecoaches, steamboats, horseback, or walking. No matter how men and women went West, they could be sure of two things. The trip would be long and uncomfortable.

During this time, wagon trains were the popular westbound means of transportation. They were

~ Trails West ~

Wagon trains usually followed two established trails to the West. Those heading for the northwest took the Oregon Trail, which was in use from about 1840 until the railroads replaced the wagon trains. The trail ran from Independence, Missouri, to the Columbia River region of Oregon. It crossed about 2,000 miles of rugged terrain, including mountains and desert. The Oregon Trail was not for the faint of heart. The entire trip took four to six months. Thousands of settlers rode the Oregon Trail in the nineteenth century, some 12,000 in the 1840s alone. In 1843, 1,000 travelers joined Marcus Whitman in the "great migration."

Born in New York in 1802, Whitman was a doctor and missionary to Native Americans in the Northwest.

In 1847, measles broke out at Whitman's mission. Because they lacked immunity, many Native Americans died of the disease. They suspected Whitman of some kind of magic, or sorcery. He, his wife, and others were killed in an attack on the settlement. This massacre resulted in a bill from Congress in 1848 that organized the Oregon Territory.

Those who were heading for the Southwest took the Santa Fe Trail. An important commercial route, it was opened

usually made up of about 100 Conestoga wagons, similar to those the Shirleys drove west. A Conestoga wagon had a white canvas top and curved sides. It could hold up to six tons of goods, and it was pulled by four to six horses. Another type of wagon was called the prairie schooner. It had lower sides than the Conestoga wagon and was named for its canvas

Pioneer camp

by trader William Becknell in 1821. It twisted and turned from Independence, Missouri, southwest to Santa Fe, New Mexico. From there, the trail divided into two branches. One branch wound up toward Utah, ending eventually in Los Angeles. The other branch went south to San Diego. It became such an important route that the United States seized New Mexico during the Mexican War (1846-48) to keep it. Traffic on the trail got heavier after the introduction of mail delivery service via stagecoach in 1849, but the traffic became obsolete in 1880 when the Santa Fe Railroad was completed.

top, which made it look from a distance like a sailing ship.

Wagon train caravans met in early spring at towns along the Mississippi or Missouri rivers. Both the Oregon Trail and the Santa Fe Trail began in Independence, Missouri, which was just over 125 miles north of Carthage, the town where Belle Starr

After the Civil War ended in 1865, hundreds of families packed up their belongings and traveled on the rugged Oregon Trail. The long trip was uncomfortable and dangerous.

lived as a child. Once a wagon train group gathered together, they chose a leader, hired guides, and bought their supplies. When the weather seemed suitable, a wagon train began its long journey protected by a few armed riders on horseback. Writes one traveler, "October 1st saw us—a wagon, three horses and our humble household necessities—bound for the 'Promised Land.' My fears vanished as we traveled toward our Mecca."

The uncomfortable, dangerous trip followed a fairly boring routine. Up at 4:00 A.M., on the trail by 7:00 A.M., moving at a snail's pace until 4:00 P.M., stopping for the night, and up again at 4:00 A.M. Not much halted the slow migration for long—not even births and deaths. Only major tragedies stopped the wagon trains—things like terrible weather, a flooded river, widespread illness, or attacks by hostile Native Americans, who sometimes viewed the trespassers on their land with justifiable anger. The danger of attack by Native Americans, however, has been exaggerated throughout history. Such attacks did occur, and they made splendid movie drama, but they were rare. Accidents probably accounted for more deaths than surprise Indian attacks. The vast majority of deaths were due to disease. Half of the deaths of all people heading West between 1840 and 1860 were due to the dreaded disease, cholera. This bacterial infection attacks the small intestine and enters the body through spoiled water or foods.

Speedy but Risky Stagecoaches

For those who favored a speedier trip than the prairie schooner, the stagecoach—which carried passengers

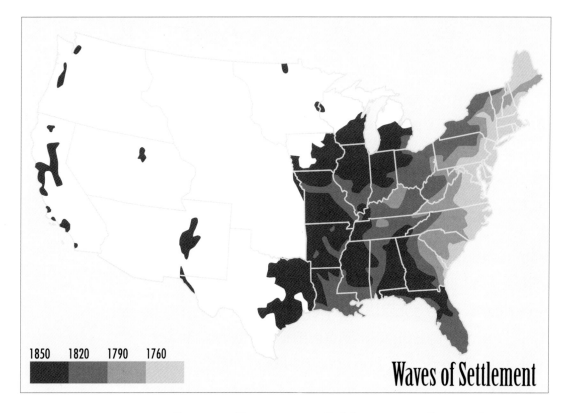

Waves of Settlement

1850   1820   1790   1760

as well as mail—was available. It was faster, but it was more cramped and uncomfortable than the covered wagon—and just as dangerous. In addition to all the normal hazards of the trail, stagecoach drivers usually drove at reckless speeds to maintain schedules.

Inside the typical stagecoach were nine seats— three in front, three in the middle, three in back. Tickets were the same price no matter where you sat. If you were a lady, you got to ride in the front seats. This was desirable because the middle seats had only a leather strap for a back, which could become uncomfortable very quickly. The rear seats were often piled high with cargo, such as sacks of flour. Rear-seat passengers might ride with boxes on their knees. Most coaches had a roof rack for baggage, and adventurous passengers were sometimes allowed to ride up there and hang on for dear life.

You never knew who your companions might be on a stagecoach ride. Well-dressed Easterners might find themselves sitting next to an unwashed character armed with a shotgun.

Sometimes the journey was livened up by runaway horses. Many things could spook the stagecoach team, which usually had three pairs of horses. When the horses became spooked, off the coach would go, driver and passengers rocketing along the bumpy trail until the team tired or the coach was dumped over.

For the stagecoach drivers, it was not an easy trip either. Unprotected in all kinds of weather, their arms grew weary from gripping the reins and holding back the wayward team. Sometimes an armed guard rode along, but the driver was often by himself on top of the coach. Some drivers relieved the stress of their jobs by drinking. There were numerous incidents, some with serious results, of drivers running into trees or falling off the stage while bouncing along at great speed.

The Elegance of Steamboats

For those who shunned the prairie schooner or the stagecoach, there was always the steamboat or the horse. Not many travelers going West for the first time were experienced enough to travel alone on horseback, but steamboat travel was considered quite elegant. A cabin, of course, could be expensive, but even a steamboat trip was wearying. Besides, travelers could not really get very far west unless they sailed the Missouri River. Rivers such as the Arkansas, Red, and Rio Grande were not navigable to the Great Plains.

Many people heading westward traveled by steamboat on the Missouri River. Travelers considered the steamboat a more elegant form of transportation.

Except for the wagon trains, most westbound travelers stopped at hotels along the trail. These were not
fancy places, but they were a welcome relief from the
tiring journey. When the westward boom began,
there was a scramble to build hotels. Some places,
such as Kansas City, ended up with too many.
Generally, however, there was a shortage of rooms at
the inns in smaller, frontier towns.

Anyone traveling west, by whatever means, was
always interested in the latest news. After the war,
rumors began to spread that some former Quantrill
followers had formed their own robber band. And so
began the legends of the James boys and the
Younger brothers. These notorious outlaws would
become entwined with the legends surrounding
Belle Starr.

Chapter 3

TURBULENT TIMES

THE TEEN QUEEN

S tories about the wild exploits of the James gang reached the Shirley home in Texas. John Shirley was especially interested in news of their comings and goings because the Younger boys were part of the gang. Shirley had known Cole, the oldest of the Younger brothers, back in Missouri.

The four Youngers might not have received the romantic press given to Frank and Jesse James, but they were no slouches either. Thomas Coleman

Jesse James was one of the most notorious outlaws of the Wild West.

"Cole" Younger, the oldest, was born in Missouri at Lee's Summit, in 1844. When he joined Quantrill's raiders, he met Frank James. After the war, Cole joined the James gang formed by Frank and his brother Jesse. In the summer of 1866, some of the gang, Jesse and Cole among them, were heading back to Missouri from San Antonio, Texas. On their way, they stopped at the Shirley home in Texas to renew old acquaintances.

Jesse and Cole stayed on the farm for a while. Belle was eighteen. Supposedly, Belle and Cole began a romance. Long after Cole had headed north, Belle told her parents that she was going to have a child. They were not pleased.

Marriage and a Child

Belle's baby, a girl she called Rose Pearl, was born sometime between 1867 and 1869 at the Shirley farm—or so the stories go. Belle supposedly called the baby Pearl Younger. However, in his autobiography, Cole Younger denies the romance. He claims to have visited the Shirley farm in 1864, not 1866. Cole recalls that sometime later, Belle (whom he called Myra), married her old boyfriend, Jim Reed.

~ THE YOUNGER BROTHERS ~

The Younger boys had witnessed the bloody fights over slavery along the Kansas-Missouri border. After the Civil War, Cole was the first to join the James gang. By 1872, all four Younger brothers—Cole, John, Jim, and Bob—were in the bank-robbing business. Soon they were robbing trains, too.

John was the first of the Younger brothers to die. He was killed in a shoot-out with Pinkerton detectives in 1874. The criminal careers of the three remaining Youngers came to an end two years later. As part of the James gang, they were captured at a bank hold-up in Northfield, Minnesota. All three were sent to prison, where Bob died of tuberculosis. The two remaining brothers were pardoned in 1901. Jim, who had been badly wounded in the Northfield job, put a bullet through his head the next year. After Cole served a prison sentence of more than 20 years, he toured with some Wild West shows and wrote an autobiography in 1903 called *The Story of Cole Younger*. Cole died in Missouri in 1916.

Myra Belle Shirley and James C. Reed were indeed married on November 1, 1866. Belle was eighteen, and Jim was twenty. Before Jim arrived in Texas, Belle had last seen him when he was part of Quantrill's band. When Jim's father died, his mother had moved the family to Texas. There, the family had renewed an old friendship with the Shirleys.

According to the marriage license, Belle Shirley and Jim Reed were wed in Collin County by Reverend S.M. Wilkins. For a time, Reed stayed on the Shirley farm, but he and Belle later returned to Missouri, where it is said that Belle and Jim's daughter, Rosie Lee, was born in September 1868. The family called her Pearl.

Not surprisingly, there are many versions of Belle's marriage to Reed. One story tells of a splendidly fancy wedding ceremony on horseback. Reed had to get out of Texas as soon as possible because there was a "price on his head" (he was a wanted man). An outlaw friend supposedly held the reins of the horses to keep them steady. After the ceremony, Reed dashed back to Missouri and safety while Belle returned to her family's farm. As exciting as the story sounds, it probably isn't true. Jim Reed was, in fact, not a wanted man in Texas. He had fought for the Confederacy, which was certainly no disgrace in Texas!

Another equally fanciful tale says that Jim Reed actually joined the Confederate army after serving with Quantrill. In 1866, Jim went to the Shirley farm to ask for Belle's hand in marriage, but her father said no. The couple was married in secret—also on horseback—after which Reed left and Belle's father sent her off to school in another county. Supposedly, Reed found her there and took his bride back to Missouri where Pearl was born.

A Brother's Death

Whatever the true details of her marriage, Belle's happiness was soon overshadowed by news of her brother Edwin's death. A year younger than Belle, Edwin apparently stole horses for a living. In fact, Edwin had become quite good at it, According to *The Dallas News*, Edwin's reputation was his undoing. He was shot off his horse and killed by Texas law officers in the fall of 1868. That left the Shirleys with two remaining sons, Mansfield, about seventeen years old, and Cravens, known as "Sugar" or "Shug," about twelve years old.

When she heard of her brother Edwin's death, Belle went to Texas with her daughter for a brief visit. After she returned to Missouri, according to one story, Belle was the perfect mother, often seen riding sidesaddle with her baby daughter in her arms.

Belle may have enjoyed being a mother, but it's hard to know if she enjoyed being a wife. Since he

OTHER FAMOUS LADIES OF THE WEST

The colorful stories of the rugged American frontier are not limited to men. Besides Belle Starr, the Wild West had its share of notorious women. One of them was Martha Jane Cannary of Mercer County, Missouri, who is far better known as Calamity Jane.

Although she was never an outlaw, Calamity Jane was certainly a "character." She could shoot, drink, and swear with the best of men. The details of her life are so filled with inventions—largely of her own making—that it is almost impossible to separate fact from fiction. Supposedly, Martha Jane got her nickname "Calamity" because she was such trouble to any man who dared to cross her. Whether panning for gold or riding shotgun on the Pony Express, no one challenged her—supposedly because she was a dead-eye shot.

According to one legend, Calamity Jane fell in love with Wild Bill Hickock, another well-known figure of the West.

Calamity Jane died of pneumonia in 1903 in Deadwood, South Dakota. Her last words were reportedly, "Bury me next to Wild Bill." And so she was.

Calamity Jane

One of the Wild West's other most famous females was a sharpshooter who went by the name of Annie Oakley. Born Phoebe Ann Moses in Ohio in 1860, she developed an amazing talent for shooting at an early age. As a young girl, she became known as "Little Sure Shot." One legend says that she could shoot wild game with such accuracy that she was able to pay off her family's mortgage with the income she earned from hunting.

At the age of 15, Annie won her first major shooting match, which gained her quick notoriety. By 1885—at the age of 25—she joined "Buffalo Bill" Cody's Wild West Show and was billled as the "Peerless Lady Wing-Shot." She was the show's main attraction for more than 16 years.

Annie Oakley's feats of marksmanship astounded audiences throughout the world. At 30 paces, she could shatter the edge of a playing card held sideways. She could hit a dime tossed in the air. And she could shoot a cigarette out of her husband's mouth. In 1887, she was presented to Queen Victoria, and later performed the cigarette trick for Crown Prince Wilhelm of Germany—with the prince holding the cigarette!

A train wreck that left her partially paralyzed in 1901 did not stop Annie Oakley. After a brief period of recovery, she returned to the stage and amazed audiences for another 25 years. She died in Greenville, Ohio on November 3, 1926.

Annie Oakley

didn't like farming and preferred gambling and racing horses, Jim Reed wasn't home all that much. Through Cole Younger and Frank James, Jim Reed met Cherokee Tom Starr. He lived west of Fort Smith, Arkansas, in an area that is now part of Oklahoma. Reed began to spend a good deal of time at the Starr ranch.

The Starr Gang

A full-blooded Cherokee, Tom Starr stood more than 6 feet 5 inches tall. He and his wife Catherine had raised a rather terrifying brood of eight boys and two girls, all of whom formed the core of the "Starr Gang." Throughout the Civil War and afterward, the Starr's land had become the most dangerous area in Indian Territory. The Starr ranch became a haven for outlaws, such as Jim Reed. By the time Tom Starr died in 1890, he had supposedly killed at least one hundred men.

The Starrs became skilled at stealing cattle and horses. It's likely that Reed got caught up in some of these escapades. That isn't what got him in trouble, however. In 1869, when Pearl was about a year old, Reed became a fugitive after he tracked down and killed the man who had supposedly murdered his brother Scott. (Scott Reed had supposedly been ambushed and killed in a case of mistaken identity.)

Because Tom Reed had a price on his head in Arkansas, he decided to head for California.

The Bandit Queen, Belle Starr, was charged with many crimes, including stealing horses.

With her outlaw husband and a young baby, Belle Shirley Reed headed to the far west. This decision to leave Texas for California brought Belle into her first serious trouble with the law. Because she was fleeing with a fugitive, Belle—once the little girl from Carthage, Missouri—became a fugitive, too.

Chapter 4

THE WILD WEST
A FUGITIVE

*L*ittle is known about Belle's life during the time she and Reed lived in California. Few records remain of the Reed's trip west, and there is little information about what happened when they got there. Some accounts say that Reed traveled west by horseback and that Belle and Pearl went by stagecoach. They settled in Los Angeles where Jim supposedly worked in a gambling house. Some accounts say they lived in a town called Los Nietos along the San Gabriel River. Perhaps there is so little known about Belle during this period because the couple was deliberately "laying low" and trying to stay out of trouble. Nobody knew Jim Reed in Los Angeles, or Belle for that matter. That suited them just fine. There the Reeds had a son, James Edwin, in 1871. Belle named him for her brother, Edwin Benton, who had been killed in 1871 in Texas.

While the Reeds were maintaining a relatively quiet lifestyle in Los Angeles, the Wild West was growing wilder. Westward migration was in full swing. Formerly sleepy towns such as Tombstone, Arizona, and Abilene, Kansas, came alive with the sounds of gunfire as outlaws and lawmen fought it out in the dusty streets.

Difficult, Disorganized, and Dirty

But the excitement of shoot-outs and showdowns was only part of the picture. Life in the American West in the 1870s was difficult, disorganized, and dirty. You were far more likely to lose your life to disease, overwork, and a lack of adequate medical care than from an outlaw's bullet. It was difficult to get food unless you grew your own. In fact, it was difficult to obtain anything unless you grew it or made it

Many saloons were the scenes of wild shoot-outs like this one.

yourself. People farmed the land with poor tools and scant knowledge of weather conditions. A white settler trying to make an honest living was often caught between the outlaws and gunmen on one side and Native Americans, who resented the intrusion, on the other.

Life in the West, no matter how difficult, was not all work, of course. Those who sought a bit of fun in their leisure hours turned to the frontier's saloons, such as the one where Jim Reed might have worked. The saloon in the Old West was the center of recreation, a restaurant, hotel, political arena, post office, ice cream parlor, gambling den, barbershop, sports arena, and dueling ground—all rolled into one.

The authority figure in the saloon was the bartender, who usually owned the place. Bartenders were in great demand. If a man came into a new boom town and wanted to build a saloon, he could be assured of many ready hands to help him. Small towns might be able to keep one saloon in business, but Dodge City, Kansas, with a population of about 1,200 in 1876, boasted 19 such establishments!

Fancy Gamblers and Jumpin' Dance Halls

A necessary addition to the saloon were the gamblers. Having learned their profession on Mississippi riverboats, many gamblers went west in the 1870s. Gamblers considered themselves generally above the "rough and ready" men of the West, and they dressed the part. They often wore black suits, fancy

Many people flocked to California during the second half of the nineteenth century. Some, like Belle and Jim Reed, were seeking a place to hide in the vastness of California. But many were seeking riches, triggered by the discovery of gold in 1848.

John Augustus Sutter was a Swiss adventurer. In 1834, he had migrated to New York City, leaving his wife and four children behind. Eventually, he found his way to the California settlement of Yerba Buena on a magnificent harbor. The settlement later became San Francisco. From there, he traveled north into the Napa Valley where he bought an old fort, in what is Sacramento today. When he decided that he needed a sawmill, he hired James Marshall, a carpenter from New Jersey, to build one.

On a rainy day in January 1848, Marshall inspected the site for the sawmill that he and his crew were building. He noticed something glittering in the streambed. "My eye was caught by something shiny in the bottom of the ditch," he recalled. "I reached my hand down and picked it up; it made my heart thump, for I was certain it was gold. The piece was about half the size and shape of a pea. Then I saw another..."

Marshall took the yellow rock to Sutter's Fort and showed Sutter a pile of tiny grains. Marshall said he believed they were gold. After a look at the *American Encyclopedia*, Sutter decided that Marshall had indeed found gold.

Augustus Sutter was a smart businessman. He was well aware that the little empire he had created would be filled with people once the word got out that California had gold. So he tried to keep the news quiet. But the news leaked out, and it was made official on December 5, 1848, when President James Polk sent this message to Congress: "The accounts of the abundance of gold in that territory are of such an extraordinary character as would scarcely command belief were they not corroborated by the authentic reports of officers in the public service."

The Gold Rush had begun. "The blacksmith dropped his hammer, the farmer his sickle, the baker his loaf," an official in nearby Monterey wrote. "All were off for the mines, some on horses, some on carts, and some on crutches..."

And what a rush it was! It's uncertain just how many migrated to California in the hope of getting rich on gold. However, in just four years, from 1848 until 1852, the non-Native American population of California increased from some 14,000 to more than 220,000!

People who went to California were called "forty-niners," which referred to the year most people rushed west to find gold. At first, gold was easy to find. It could even be scooped out of the rivers with spoons. Eventually, there was little easy gold left. Most of the money was made by those who provided services to the miners. Levi Strauss made jeans. Wells, Fargo and Company started a banking firm. Others opened hotels and supply stores. Still others got rich feeding the miners.

The gold rush, with all the forty-niners, changed California. In 1850, California became part of the Union as a free state.

This cartoon shows money-crazed people rushing to California for gold.

THE WAY THEY GO TO CALIFORNIA.

frilled shirts, and an a great deal of flashy jewelry. This was partly for the benefit of the local bettors who seemed to prefer losing their money to a well-dressed stranger than to someone clad in buckskin breeches just like themselves. The gambler's stay in any one place was usually short, depending on the saloon itself and the clientele willing to bet—and usually lose—their money.

The better, more elegant gamblers became quite well known throughout the West. These people could improve a town's reputation just by entering it. When an army of gamblers went to Benton near Medicine Bow in Wyoming, in only two weeks the sleepy town's population jumped to 3,000, as newcomers filled its twenty-three brand-new saloons and five dance halls!

Dance halls weren't just places to watch pretty girls dance. They were places where cowboys could kick up their heels, too. Dancing was a popular form of entertainment, mostly because it was cheap. It also gave men and women a chance to enjoy one another's company. And, if there didn't happen to be any women around, cowboys would dance with one another just for the fun of dancing. Nobody dared to laugh.

The waltz was a favorite dance in California halls. Other Western regions to the east preferred the square dance. Towns along the Mississippi often moved to the sound of the fiddle. Towns in the Southwest were influenced by Mexican culture. Ladies sat on benches around the room, dressed in their finery. A gentleman approached the lady of his choice and asked for a dance. The lady could either accept or decline as she wished. After each dance, it was proper for the gentleman to offer the lady some refreshment, perhaps a sweet cake of some sort.

Happiness in California

For Belle, California's open spaces and its anonymity made this one of the happiest periods in her life. In a letter to her brother Marion in 1872, she wrote (spellings and punctuation are hers):

> *Dear Brother Marion,*
> *I take my pen in hand to write you a few lines this morning. We are all enjoying the best of health. Indeed it is a rare thing for any one to be sick in this country. . . . I presume you would like to hear how we have been getting along lately.*

When we left San Bernardino we rented a place in Los Nietos. Los Nietos is an island as is said to be best location in California . . . . Jimmie has bought land here on this island and I guess we will make a permanent home here. I am perfectly satisfied. I think in a few years we can have as lovely a place as this state can boast of . . . . Rosie sends her love to all. I haven't written to Prest yet . . . . Write soon Marion and give us all the news. Give my love to all and I want them all to write soon and often.

In haste,
MAY

If the Reeds had gotten away with their quiet life and stayed in California, perhaps the world would never have heard of them again. But Jim Reed just could not stay out of trouble. This time federal agents got after him for passing bad checks. While looking into that matter, they discovered he was wanted for murder in Arkansas. Now, Texas—not California—began to look like the safest place for the couple.

Fleeing Back to Texas

So, the Reeds went back to Texas. Once again, almost nothing is known of their trek back home. Most accounts say that Reed returned to Texas on horseback. Accounts vary on whether Belle returned with the children by either stagecoach or by ship around Cape Horn.

Much more is known about Belle's life once the Reeds were back in Texas. The Reeds lived in Scyene or near the Shirley ranch, although Jim was at home only for brief periods. He spent most of his time hiding from the law in Indian Territory at Tom Starr's place. On occasion, he would get word to Belle to meet him at some designated spot. She would then leave the children with her mother and ride off to be with her fugitive husband. If that is true, then perhaps it's also true that young Sam Starr, Tom's son and Belle's future husband, would sometimes accompany them.

A story in *The Dallas Commercial* claimed that the Reeds bought a farm on Coon Creek in Bosque County, Texas. According to that report, Jim Reed hung out with all kinds of horse thieves and desperadoes. In February 1873, four men robbed and killed a man named Dick Cravery. He and his brother Sol were two of the murderers. In August of the same year, Jim and Sol murdered another man named Wheeler, who had once been a gang member of theirs. After they committed another murder, the citizens ran them out of town.

Sol fled to Missouri, and Jim was now wanted for murder in both Arkansas and Texas. Leaving the children with their grandparents, Reed and Belle sought a hideout at the Starr ranch. For the first time, Belle might have seen the large and beautiful bend in the South Canadian River that would later become her last home.

Belle in Buckskins

Belle's adventures during this period are most likely what earned her the reputation as the Bandit Queen. In late 1873, Reed and his gang robbed a wealthy farmer and stock dealer, Watt Grayson, of some $30,000 in gold. It is said that Belle, dressed as a man, aided her husband in the robbery. However, there are no newspaper accounts that include Belle among the robbers, and no one in the Grayson family who witnessed the robbery identified her.

There are some fascinating tales about Belle during this period. Although it was probably a case of guilt by association, she was reportedly seen in all the "best" hotels in Dallas while her husband was in hiding. She dressed in buckskins and a man's Stetson hat decorated with an ostrich plume. Her cartridge belt had twin revolvers. She drank in saloons with her foot propped up on the brass rail. She gambled. And she adored being known as the Bandit Queen.

One thing is fairly certain. The seven-year marriage of Belle and Jim Reed was in trouble. It might have been that Belle had grown tired of life on the run. It might have been that she did not like having a lawbreaker for a husband. Most likely, she did not fancy a husband who took off for San Antonio with an eighteen-year-old girl named Rosa McComus!

On April 7, 1874, the San Antonio stagecoach was robbed in broad daylight. Three men—one of them Jim Reed—got away with about $2,500 and four gold watches. Surprisingly, stagecoach robbery was still a fairly new crime in Texas. People were outraged. A $7,000 reward was offered. Rosa McComus was brought in for questioning, but she was released because she had no part in the robbery.

"A Destitute Condition"

Even for the most daring and successful of outlaws, life eventually ended in violence. So it ended for James C. Reed. He was shot and killed on August 6, 1874, near Paris, Texas, by John T. Morris, his distant relative. Morris, a special deputy, had been tracking Reed since the stage robbery. The news-papers related the story that Morris and Reed had been traveling together and had stopped at a farmhouse for dinner. While they were seated, Morris asked Reed to stand up and surrender. Instead, Reed ducked under the table. Morris fired through the table, killing Reed.

Belle was later questioned by federal marshals about the Grayson robbery. The records say she had no active role. Some historians say she refused to identify that the body as her husband's so that Morris would not get the reward. In testimony given to the Commissioner of Indian Affairs in December 1875, she said that Reed and his accomplices showed up after the robbery and counted the money in front of her. As for what happened to it, she said that "no part could be recovered, my said husband having spent or disposed of all that he had and having left me in a destitute condition."

Belle wrote a letter to her late husband's family in August of 1876. In it, she said that she had more trouble than any other person. Indeed, she had a point. Her father died in Scyene that June, and her mother moved to Dallas. Her youngest brother, Shug, was now eighteen and had to leave home because, like his brothers, he was in trouble with the law. Young Eddie got sick, and Belle sent him to his grandparents, the Reeds, where he lived until he was twelve. The farm wasn't making much money, and poor Belle didn't know where to turn next.

Chapter 5

INDIAN TERRITORY

STARR TIME

After Reed's death, the only bright spot left in Belle's life was her daughter Pearl. Belle sent her to school in Dallas and told the Reeds that the child had gained a worldwide reputation in the theater for her dancing ability. That is probably a hefty exaggeration fueled by a mother's pride. One of Belle's biographers says that Pearl's reputation was "local," not worldwide. In any event, the child suffered a fainting spell on stage during a performance, and Belle kept her out of the theater after that.

Rumors About Belle

From then until the end of the 1870s, what the Bandit Queen did and where she went is somewhat of a mystery. There is, however, no scarcity of theories.

One particularly exciting account has Belle leaving Pearl with an old schoolmate in Conway, Arkansas. Then, Belle returned to Dallas where she quite unintentionally set fire to a small store. She had no money to repay the damage, so she was put on trial for arson. But an old friend of her father's, a wealthy stock dealer and possible admirer, heard of her plight. He gave her money, and she was released.

Belle retrieved Pearl from Arkansas and apparently went through the money that was given her. She was soon broke again. One day, she entered a bank where the cashier was "an admirer." After some friendly chitchat, Belle whipped out a pistol from her skirt and forced the terrified suitor to give her $30,000 in a sack. She then told the cashier to keep quiet as she fled to a stable and her awaiting horse. From there, Belle rode away "like the wind."

About a year later, Belle ended up in a Dallas jail for horse stealing. However, the deputy sheriff took a liking to Belle and eloped with her.

If these stories are true, Belle was certainly busy at the end of the 1870s. She was seen in gambling halls all over the Southwest and was reportedly involved with one handsome or rich man after another. Men were obviously attracted to her, but they feared her as well. That's because she could "outride and out-shoot them all." During this time, she was known as the Bandit Queen, the Prairie Queen, and Queen of the Desperados.

One of the men in her life during this period, supposedly, was Bruce Younger, half-brother to Cole Younger's father. One report said Belle and Bruce were married in Coffeyville, Kansas, in 1878, and that's how Pearl became Pearl Younger. If, in fact, Bruce was Belle's second husband, the marriage did not last very long.

It is possible that during this time, married or not, Belle and Bruce Younger returned to Indian Territory and the Starr ranch. There, once again, she would have seen Tom Starr's son, Sam.

A New Husband

According to the records of the Cherokee Nation, Sam Starr and Maybelle Reed were married in the early summer of 1880. The entry from the Cherokee records reads as follows:

> *On the 5th day of June 1880 by Abe Woodall–District Judge for Canadian Dist. C.N. Samuel Starr, a citizen of Cherokee Nation age 23 years, and Mrs. Bell Reed, a citizen of United States age 27 years.*
>
> *H.J. Vann, Clerk.*

Interestingly enough, Myra Belle Shirley Reed Starr had dropped five years from her age when she married Starr! He was a handsome man, three-quarters Cherokee, described as having magnetic eyes. He had long, black hair, which he wore tied with a red ribbon under a broad-brimmed black hat. Although he was shorter than his father, Sam looked older than his age of twenty-three. That was probably just as well since his new wife—despite what appeared on the marriage certificate—was about nine years older than he was.

Belle and Sam settled down on sixty acres of land near a great U-shaped bend in the South Canadian River. Belle named it Youngers' Bend. The land was

A RELIGIOUS MIGRATION

Another famous westward migration took place a few years after the Cherokee's march. This was the trek to Utah taken by members of the Church of Jesus Christ of Latter-day Saints, more commonly known as Mormons.

Joseph Smith Jr. was a New York farmhand who claimed to have been visited by the angel Moroni. The angel gave Smith golden plates from which he translated what he called *The Book of Mormon*. Thus he founded the Mormon church in 1830. It quickly gained thousands of converts. The Mormon religion held beliefs that were different from more traditional faiths. The fact that Smith approved the practice of polygamy, allowing a man to have more than one wife at the same time, set them even further apart from other Americans. Regarded as odd—and even dangerous—the Mormons isolated themselves in tightly knit communities. Constant harassment from neighbors kept them on the move.

As their numbers constantly increased, the Mormons first settled in Kirtland, Ohio, and Independence, Missouri, and then in the

Joseph Smith, Jr.

newly formed town of Nauvoo, Illinois. Here, Smith and his brother Hyrum were killed by an angry mob hoping to break up the church.

It was time to leave once again. The new Mormon leader was Brigham Young, a carpenter from Vermont and a stern and capable administrator who had joined the Mormons in 1832. Young had his own vision for the Latter-Day Saints, and it lay west. In the wilderness, on the other side of the Rocky Mountains, Young envisioned a new community where the Mormons could live in peace and practice their religion without fear.

In February 1846, a remarkable journey of some 15,000 Mormons began. From Nauvoo, Illinois, they headed west across the Mississippi. Some 600 of them died either of disease or from a dwindling fuel supply that winter. Young went ahead with a small scouting party. He had heard of a beautiful valley in the western Rockies, called the valley of the Great Salt Lake. It is said that when Young actually saw the site that would become Salt Lake City, Utah, he exclaimed, "This is the place."

In 1847, the Mormons reached the "promised land," which they called the state of Deseret. They vowed to make the desert bloom. In 1848, The Salt Lake Valley became part of the United States after the war with Mexico. Young became the governor of the territory in 1851. Utah became a state in 1896. Today, Mormons number around 5 million members.

Mormon pioneers

not actually theirs. Cherokee land was held by all Cherokees. A Cherokee might choose a parcel of land and if no one else claimed it he could keep it for a lifetime. With her marriage, Belle was now a member of the Cherokee Nation.

The Trail of Tears

Sadly, no matter how they tried to fit in, the Cherokee were at the mercy of the land-hungry U.S. settlers. When gold was discovered on Cherokee land in Georgia, the end for the nation was near. In 1835, a small number of Cherokee were forced to give up all their land east of the Mississippi River for 5 million dollars. The rest of the Cherokee nation denounced the treaty and took their case to the U.S. Supreme Court. They won. The Court declared that Georgia had no claims to Cherokee holdings.

The decision hardly mattered. President Andrew Jackson had little use for Native Americans and treated them without honor. He would not enforce the Supreme Court's decision, and Georgia's leaders simply ignored it.

What followed was one of the more shameful acts in American history. Some 15,000 Cherokee were driven

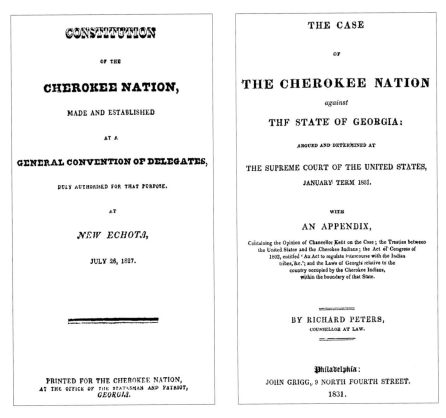

CONSTITUTION

OF THE

CHEROKEE NATION,

MADE AND ESTABLISHED

AT A

GENERAL CONVENTION OF DELEGATES,

DULY AUTHORISED FOR THAT PURPOSE.

AT

NEW ECHOTA,

JULY 26, 1827.

PRINTED FOR THE CHEROKEE NATION,
AT THE OFFICE OF THE STATESMAN AND PATRIOT,
GEORGIA.

THE CASE

OF

THE CHEROKEE NATION

against

THE STATE OF GEORGIA:

ARGUED AND DETERMINED AT

THE SUPREME COURT OF THE UNITED STATES,

JANUARY TERM 1831.

WITH

AN APPENDIX,

Containing the Opinion of Chancellor Kent on the Case ; the Treaties between
the United States and the Cherokee Indians ; the Act of Congress of
1802, entitled ' An Act to regulate intercourse with the Indian
tribes, &c.'; and the Laws of Georgia relative to the
country occupied by the Cherokee Indians,
within the boundary of that State.

BY RICHARD PETERS,
COUNSELLOR AT LAW.

Philadelphia:
JOHN GRIGG, 9 NORTH FOURTH STREET.
1831.

In 1838, the U. S. government forced thousands of Cherokee off their land in Georgia and ordered them to go to Oklahoma. The Cherokee's journey is commonly known as the "Trail of Tears."

from their land and sent west on a forced march during the fall and winter of 1838–39. This migration became known as the Trail of Tears. Accompanied by 7,000 U.S. troops, and with inadequate food supplies, some 4,000 Cherokee died on the miserable 116-day journey to northeastern Oklahoma.

For about the next 75 years, the Cherokee lived on land "given to them" by the U.S. government. They were joined by members of the Creek, Chickasaw, Choctaw, and Seminole nations, who had also been driven from their lands in the Southeast. When Oklahoma was about to become a state in 1907, some of the land was given to the Native Americans. The rest was opened up to white settlers.

ᕯ THE CHEROKEE NATION ᕯ

The Cherokee people had once lived around the Great Lakes, but had migrated to eastern Tennessee and the western Carolinas. When the British began to colonize the New World, the Cherokee were helpful to them. As more settlers entered the area, the Cherokee began to lose their hunting grounds.

When the American Revolution began, the Cherokee sided with the British. Cherokee attacks on U.S. forts only brought more attacks from the Americans.

When the American Revolution ended in 1783, the Cherokee made a remarkable attempt to fit in with the new United States of America. They aided future president Andrew Jackson in his fight against the Creek nation. They modeled their government after the U.S. Constitution. Most remarkable of all, one of their own, Sequoyah, who had served in the U.S. Army, developed a system of writing. In a short time, most of the Cherokee nation was literate.

About 45,000 descendants of the Cherokee live in eastern Oklahoma today. Some of them still live on land allotted to them after the Trail of Tears. Belle's father-in-law, Tom Starr, did not belong to the Cherokees who had taken that terrible journey. His family had migrated west about a year or two earlier, settling in a place Belle would call home.

A Quiet Life

Also settling in at Youngers' Bend was Belle's eleven-year-old daughter, now called Pearl Starr. The new family settled down to what seemed like a quiet life. They decorated the cabin—and they even built a shelf for some of Father Shirley's old books and brought in a piano from St. Louis. They planted crops and built a smokehouse. In their spare time, Belle and Sam, according to some stories, dug holes around the cabin. Rumor had it that a Cherokee named Big Head had buried thousands of dollars in gold coins when he had lived there after the Civil War. If so, no money was ever found.

The Starrs were not exactly neighborly people, although they were surrounded by Sam's relatives. The only entrance to Youngers' Bend was by a

THE JAMES GANG

Alexander Franklin James and Jesse Woodson James were born in Missouri—Frank in 1843, and Jesse in 1847. They were farm boys who shared a love of guns and a strong loyalty to the South. When the Civil War began in 1861, Frank joined Quantrill's bushwhackers and took part in murderous raids along the Kansas-Missouri border.

When the war ended, most members of these guerrilla bands went home along with the regular soldiers. But not the James brothers. Jesse, supposedly, was wounded by northern soldiers even though he was carrying a white flag of truce. This apparently nudged him further along the criminal path. The James boys and eight others formed their own outlaw band and began a deadly crime wave. It started in Liberty, Missouri, on February 13,1866. With Jesse still recovering from his wounds, Frank along with Cole, Bob, and Jim Younger hit the Liberty bank and got away with $60,000. They killed an innocent bystander during the robbery. This was the first daytime bank robbery in the United States.

During the next sixteen years, the James brothers murdered at least 16 bank tellers and railroad workers as they robbed a dozen banks, seven trains, and three stagecoaches across six states.

Despite their record of crimes in Missouri, Jesse and Frank were "heroes" to the locals because they stood up to the Yankees. Missourians cheered their exploits, calling them champions for the Southern cause. Indeed, it was said that, with the money he robbed, Jesse paid off the mortgages on countless farms for widows whose husbands had been killed by Union troops.

In 1875, Pinkerton agents went to the James's family farm and tossed a flare through the window. Jesse's mother was badly injured, and his young half-brother was killed. The following year, six of the James gang were killed or captured during a robbery at the First National Bank in Northfield, Minnesota. Only Frank and Jesse escaped.

By 1879, the James brothers were back in the robbery business. The governor, Thomas T. Crittenden, offered a $10,000 reward for the brothers—dead or alive.

Jesse decided to retire. Calling himself Thomas Howard, Jesse James took his wife and two children to St. Joseph, Missouri, to settle down. On April 3, 1882, Jesse took off his guns—something he rarely did—while he straightened a picture on the wall of his home. He was shot in the back of the head.

Frank James gave himself up a few months after Jesse's death. He stood trial in Missouri, once for murder and once for robbery. Frank was found innocent. Frank James went home to Missouri. To earn money, he gave tours of Jesse's gravesite. Frank died in 1915.

The James gang

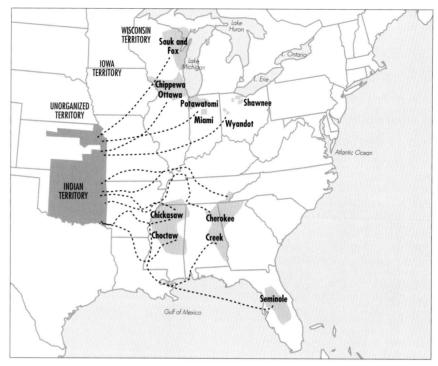

Indian Removals, 1820–1840

canyon so narrow that a wagon could barely pass through it. Belle wrote in a letter that, with her new marriage, she wished to lead a quiet life: "... I have been estranged from the society of women (whom I thoroughly detest) ... so I selected a place that few have ever had the gratification of gossiping around." But apparently the gossips were busy anyway, and Belle was shocked that anyone would find something in her past to gossip about: "It soon became noised around that I was a woman of some notoriety from Texas, and from that time on, my home and actions have been severely criticized."

Yet, she didn't find it odd when a famous outlaw came to call, even though she neglected to tell Sam his true identity. "Jesse James first came in and remained several weeks. He was unknown to my husband, and he never knew till long afterwards that our home had been honored by James' presence. I introduced Jesse as one Mr. Williams from Texas." It's possible that Jesse James visited the Starr ranch after a robbery in September 1881 and before he moved his family to St. Joseph, Missouri, in November.

Chapter 6

STEALIN' AND ROBBIN'
THE BANDIT QUEEN

etween June of 1880 and July of 1882, Belle Starr became the leader of a gang of horse thieves and killers, using Youngers' Bend as their hideout. So many outlaws used the place as a refuge that Belle and Sam were supposedly forced to build two extra cabins to accommodate them! Another story says that Belle and Sam outfitted a nearby cave for the many outlaws who stopped at Younger's Bend. The horse-stealing business was so successful that Belle

~ Robbers Cave, Oklahoma ~

There are many tourist spots in the area supposedly used by the Bandit Queen. One of the most famous is Robbers Cave in the wilderness of the San Bois Mountains in Latimer County, Oklahoma. Today, it sits in an 8,400-acre game preserve. This cave was used by army deserters as a hideout during the Civil War and might have also been used by the James and Younger gang as they traveled back and forth to Texas. But there is no proof that Belle Starr ever used it as a hideout. Nonetheless, the legend it is part of continues to attract tourists to the area.

set up stations fifty miles apart to exchange animals coming from north or south. One especially fanciful tale says that Belle once had a blacksmith nail her own horse's shoes on backward so the oncoming posse would think she had gone the other way! The Starrs also made whiskey illegally at their compound, which they sold to the Cherokees. Supposedly, they also supplied the nearby cattletown of Catoosa where saloons were prohibited.

A Warrant for the Starrs

Between 1880 and 1882, some say a reward of
$10,000 was offered for Belle and Sam Starr—dead
or alive. This appears to be true for on July 31, 1882,
a warrant was issued for their arrest. They were
charged with stealing horses from Andrew Pleasant
Crane, a Cherokee.

In September, the Starrs were reported heading for
safety in the Osage hills of Oklahoma. The deputy
marshals trailed them and captured Sam along with a
young boy whose family the Starrs had been visiting.
They sent the boy to find Belle, threatening him with
death if he told her anything but the fact that Sam
needed her. It worked, and Belle was captured, too.
It was her first arrest.

Belle on Trial

It took some weeks to get Belle and Sam Starr to the
federal courthouse in Fort Smith, Arkansas, where
they were to be tried. Along the way, Belle did every-
thing she could to escape. Supposedly, she even
grabbed a pistol from one of the guards and would
have shot him had others not stopped her.

The Starrs arrived in Fort Smith in October and immediately hired a lawyer from the firm of Cravens & Marcum. But, getting a case before an actual judge took some time. The trial finally began on February 15, 1883, presided over by Isaac C. Parker. This could not have been good news for Belle Starr. Parker, known as the "hanging" judge, was determined to bring law and order to the Indian Territory.

With the "hanging" judge on the bench and the Bandit Queen on trial, the case drew much local interest. The newspaper, Fort Smith New Era, carried this story: "In the U.S. district court last week the case of Sam Starr and Belle Starr, his wife, of the Cherokee Nation, charged with the larceny of two horses on the 20th April, 1882....The very idea of a woman being charged with an offense of this kind and that she was the leader of a band of horse thieves and wielding a power over them as their queen and guiding spirit, was sufficient to fill the courtroom with spectators."

After noting that Belle was an excellent rider and an expert with the pistol, the paper did a little editorializing. It added: "...while she could not be considered even a good-looking woman, her appearance is of that kind as would be sure to attract the attention of wild and desperate characters."

Belle never took the witness stand, but Sam did. The trial lasted four days. The Starrs' defense was that old Tom Starr had the measles and that Belle and Sam were at his bedside during the week of the accused horse stealing. However, when cross-examined, no one was exactly sure of the dates. Even Tom Starr had to admit that "Indians go by the moon."

The jury did not buy the measles defense. They took just one hour to turn in their verdict—Belle and Sam Starr were found guilty. Perhaps the hanging judge was in a good mood that day. He gave them a relatively light sentence—a year in prison in Detroit, Michigan. The judge said that they could be paroled in nine months for good behavior and that he hoped after that they would become "decent citizens." It is even felt that Judge Parker admired Belle Starr because she was a fighter for Indian rights, something he himself believed in.

A Model Prisoner

After sending her daughter to live with friends in Kansas, Belle and Sam boarded a railroad prison car

Belle Starr was known as an excellent horsewoman. She usually wore a black velvet riding habit, a man's wide hat, and a Colt .45 on her waist.

STEALIN' AND ROBBIN': THE BANDIT QUEEN

and headed for the House of Correction in Detroit, Michigan. They spent nine months in prison. Some historians claim Belle was not only a model prisoner but apparently something of a celebrity behind bars. They say she became the warden's assistant, taught his children the piano, and discussed current literature with other prison officials.

However Belle passed the time behind bars, she and Sam were released by the end of the year, and they headed home. They stopped to pick up Pearl in Missouri. Mabel Harrison, an orphan who was related to the Reeds, had become Pearl's good friend while her mother was away. Belle took both girls back to Youngers' Bend to live. Belle's twelve-year-old son Eddie was at his grandmother's in Texas. They settled into a quiet life as farmers. Belle often took off for Fort Smith leaving Pearl at home to take care of Eddie.

Belle Starr was now thirty-five years old. With her long black hair and deep tan, some thought she was of Native American ancestry. An excellent horsewoman, she liked to wear a black velvet riding habit and a man's wide hat. She usually had a Colt .45 strapped to her waist. And she was not shy about using it. Despite her outward appearances, Belle was apparently still quite concerned about "remaining feminine." That is why she never smoked cigars, as some western women did. According to one story, she could get downright difficult about being treated correctly. It's said that one day her hat blew off while she was riding. She asked a man, also on horseback, to retrieve it. He didn't. Instantly, she whipped out her gun and pointed it between his eyes. He jumped off his horse for the hat. Belle said, "The next time a *lady* asks you to pick up her hat, do as she tells you."

Life at Youngers' Bend

Belle, Sam, and the girls settled down in Youngers' Bend. There was spring planting and school in nearby Briartown for the girls. But life was apparently not all quiet bliss. Belle was seen in the Fort Smith gambling halls playing for the highest stakes. It is said that she would sometimes drop into a saloon and play the piano for hours, with the wide eyes of small boys and girls staring at this notorious woman with guns strapped to her waist. It's also said that Belle's gang was operating again, stealing horses and livestock in Arkansas and Kansas.

Perhaps the real reason that life was disrupted at Youngers' Bend was a man with the odd name of Blue Duck. Belle Starr apparently became quite "taken" with this member of a small-time gang of rustlers and stage robbers. It is not known what Sam thought about Blue Duck, but he might well have been pleased when the outlaw was sent off to the prison for life after killing a farmer on a drunken spree in 1884.

Unfortunately for Sam, his marriage troubles did not stop with Blue Duck's imprisonment. John Middleton, aged 29, was wanted for murder when he stopped at Youngers' Bend in late 1884. Middleton was the late Jim Reed's cousin, and Belle had probably met him before.

Known as a daring outlaw, Middleton sported a sandy-colored mustache and dressed in a rather dandy fashion, which probably pleased Belle Starr. She and Middleton reportedly began a romance.

It is not known what Sam thought of this, or if Belle planned to leave Youngers' Bend with Middleton. The problem was taken care of, however, in May of 1885. The body of a well-dressed man with a sandy colored mustache was found a few miles from Youngers' Bend.

~ THE HANGING JUDGE ~

Isaac C. Parker was born in Ohio and was admitted to the bar in 1859, the same year he moved to St. Joseph, Missouri. In 1875, he was appointed federal judge for the Western District of Arkansas. Parker's whole purpose in life seems to have been an attempt to singlehandedly end the lawlessness in the West. To do this, he appointed 200 deputies to bring in outlaws and troublemakers. In just one day—September 3, 1875—he sentenced six men—three whites, one black, and two Cherokees—to death. By nightfall, they were swinging from the end of ropes. After that, he was known as the "hanging" judge. Parker spent twenty-one years trying cases in Fort Smith. He sent a total of eighty-seven men to the gallows. All of them had been convicted of rape or murder. Judge Parker died in 1896. Today, the gallows at Fort Smith have been reconstructed to look just like they did in the days of the hanging judge.

Some reports say John Middleton drowned. Others say he had taken a double blast from a shotgun.

In any event, Belle and Sam were back together again at Youngers' Bend. But it appeared that the Starrs would not have time to think about their obviously troubled marriage.

More Trouble for Belle

In October 1855, three men broke into a store and post office owned by Andrew J. Moore. Sam Starr and two others were charged with the break-in. Belle stoutly declared that her husband had no part in the robbery. Just to be on the safe side, Sam stayed mostly out of sight in the wilderness around Youngers' Bend.

Lawman John West, who was a Native American, tried to persuade Belle to convince her husband to surrender. Belle, of course, wouldn't hear of it. Then, in January 1886, she learned that a complaint had been filed against her for stealing a horse from Albert McCarty, a rancher. Although she surrendered to a U.S. marshall in Fort Smith and was charged with larceny, it was believed that West charged Belle to make Sam surrender. If so, it didn't work. Belle posted bond and went home to Younger's Bend to await trial.

There was more trouble for the Starrs in February. Three robbers with guns struck at the home of Wilse W. Farrill and his sons. Although the Farrill's could not identify them, a neighbor said that one of the gunmen "was a woman dressed like a man." A new complaint was filed—this time accusing Belle Starr of

Belle Starr might have had a love interest in Blue Duck (left). But, Blue Duck was sent to jail for life after killing a farmer in 1884.

STEALIN' AND ROBBIN': THE BANDIT QUEEN

being the gang's leader. Once again, Belle protested her innocence, saying she attended a dance on the night of the robbery. Once again, she posted bond and, after a few days of shopping in Fort Smith, went home to await trial.

The Farrill robbery trial took place in June. As it turned out, nobody could identify the robbers. The case was dismissed.

There was still the charge against Belle of horse stealing. That trial took place in September. Once again, the case was dismissed. A witness testified that he had seen John Middleton pay for McCarty's horse, so Belle could not possibly have stolen it.

Belle Starr returned to Younger's Bend where she found that her husband had been badly wounded in a shoot-out with the law. While she nursed him back to health, she tried to persuade him to give himself up. If Sam surrendered, she reasoned, he would be tried in a "white man's" court on a charge of burglary. If he ran away again and was caught by lawman in the West, he would be tried in a Cherokee court. Neighboring Cherokees were no friends of the Starrs, blaming them for enticing so many of their young men into lawlessness. It was likely that a Cherokee

Mr. Colt and His Gun

Classic Peacemaker .45. This model had a 7.5 inch barrel and sold for $17.

The gun that made a real difference in the life of the Old West and in the life of Belle Starr was the handiwork of an ingenious inventor named Samuel Colt of Hartford, Connecticut.

Born in Hartford in 1814, Colt joined the Navy as a young man. There, he carved a wooden revolver. He later used it as a model for the real thing. It was patented first in France and England and then in the United States in 1836. But it wasn't very popular. It had a single barrel and cartridge cylinder that rotated when the hammer was tripped. Its main problem was that it wasn't all that reliable.

Colt went out of business in 1842 when his manufacturing company in Paterson, New Jersey, failed. Five years later, word got around that the U.S. military had found his multishot weapons to be quite effective during the war with Mexico. Colt was back in business, building the world's largest private armory in Hartford, Connecticut.

With the help of Eli Whitney, Jr., son of the famed cotton gin inventor, Colt began manufacturing interchangeable gun parts. Colt also developed the first production line, an idea that would later become the key to the success of automobile manufacturing. His pistols were the most widely used on both sides during the Civil War.

In 1873, with the war over and the Wild West in full swing, Colt introduced his reliable six-shot, single-action model. It became the most famous and most used sidearm in the West. Ironically, it was called the Peacemaker.

court would sentence Sam to death or would make him face horrible torture.

Widowed Again

Sam Starr saw his wife's point and gave himself up in Briartown on February 6, 1886. It must have been quite a sight to the good citizens of the town to see Sam Starr surrender while his wife rode horseback behind him with her six-guns strapped to her waist.

It looked as though Belle had the right idea. Sam was out of jail on bond in November. They stayed in Fort Smith for a few days to see old Tom Starr, who was now in federal prison in Illinois for smuggling whiskey. Then Sam and Belle went home.

But there was little peace at Youngers' Bend. Sam blamed his father's arrest on lawmen John West and his brother Frank. That December, the Starrs attended a dance at a friend's home. As luck would have it, one of the other guests was Frank West. The two men exchanged verbal insults, drew guns, and then shot each other. A witness said Belle held her dead husband in her arms but did not weep.

Belle Starr was a widow for the second time. Sam was buried in the family plot near Briartown.

Chapter 7

THE END OF AN ERA
"A DESPERATE WOMAN KILLED"

$\mathcal{A}$s the years passed, Belle Starr seemed quite determined to "get respectable" and the Wild West, determined or not, was becoming tamed. Belle seemed to always need a man in her life. So not long after Sam Starr's death, she took up with Bill July, a twenty-four-year-old Cherokee and "adopted" son of old Tom Starr.

The Bandit Queen might have had more than romance in mind when she invited July into her home. Since Sam had died, Belle was no longer considered a member of the Cherokee Nation, which meant she could possibly lose Youngers' Bend. Now thirty-nine years old, with hard lines marking her face and gray streaks in her black hair, Belle and Jim July settled down at Youngers' Bend.

As Belle solved one problem, she faced another. The men who interested her always seemed to be on the wrong side of the law. So, she probably was not shocked when, in the summer of 1887, July was charged with horse stealing. Since Sam's death, Belle had seemed bent on becoming respectable. She refused to pay July's bail. Friends got him out anyway, and he came home. Word got out that anyone running from the law was not welcome at Youngers' Bend.

A New Neighbor

Life at Youngers' Bend eventually settled down, marred occasionally by problems with Belle's growing children, Pearl and Eddie, who were—for a time—living with her. The West was changing. White immigrants in the area now outnumbered the Native Americans. One of the newcomers was Edgar A. Watson, a hard-faced man in his thirties. He asked Belle to lease some of her land for his corn and cotton growing. Belle didn't much like the look of him, but she did like his friendly wife. Since Belle could use the money that tenant farming would bring, she agreed to his proposal.

Over the next few months, Belle learned that Edgar Watson was wanted for murder in Florida. This made the Bandit Queen uneasy. It wasn't the murder that bothered her, but the fact that Watson was a fugitive. Belle was afraid that doing business with him would cause the Cherokee Nation to reclaim her land. She tried to return Watson's tenant money. He refused and threatened her. During the angry exchange, Belle lost her temper and mentioned the Florida murder. Pearl overheard the conversation and was fearful for her mother, but Belle just laughed and forgot about it.

Belle's Last Ride

On the morning of February 3, 1889, just two days before her birthday, Belle and Bill July parted near the town of Whitefield. They had spent the night at a friend's home. July was going on to Fort Smith for the horse stealing hearing, and Belle was headed back to Youngers' Bend. Late that afternoon she stopped at the home of Jackson Rowe for some light refreshment and conversation. She left after about half an hour. Once out of sight of the Rowe farmhouse, Belle was blown from the saddle by a shotgun blast that struck her in the back and neck. A second blast tore into her face and shoulder. Belle Starr, Bandit Queen, fell to the ground, dead.

On February 6, the following article that had originated in Fort Smith, Arkansas, appeared on the front page of The New York Times:

> *A Desperate Woman Killed*
> *Word has been received from Eufala, Indian Territory, that Belle Starr was killed there Sunday night. Belle was the wife of Cole Younger...Jim Starr, her second husband, was shot down by the side of Belle less than two years ago.*
> *Belle Starr was the most desperate woman that ever figured on the borders. She married Cole Younger directly after the war, but left him and joined a band of outlaws that operated in the Indian Territory. She had been arrested for murder and robbery a score of times, but always managed to escape.*

When word reached Jim July in Fort Smith that Belle had been murdered, he vowed that "somebody would suffer." Immediately, he returned to Youngers' Bend. Watson was arrested and appeared before a Grand Jury. He protested his innocence. July was unable to produce evidence against Watson, and he was acquitted.

Had Pearl told the Grand Jury of the conversation she had overheard between Belle and Watson, the outcome might have been different. But Belle's daughter was too frightened. There was no further search for Belle's killer.

An Unsolved Mystery

Just as most facts about Belle Starr's life are questionable, so is her death. Was Watson really the murderer? Some believe Tom Starr killed his daughter-in-law because he held her responsible for Sam's life of crime. Others say a brother of Jim Reed, Belle's first husband, killed her for supposedly talking too much about Jim's whereabouts, which led to his capture and death.

Another theory states that rancher and neighbor, Hi Early, had one of his hired hands kill Belle because she shot at him after he complained she was stealing his horses. Another suspect is Jim Middleton, brother of John, Belle's old flame. Jim said Belle had hired someone to kill John so she could keep his share of the money after a robbery.

Maybe Jim July Starr killed his wife with the help of Edgar Watson. Why? Some say it was because she had caught him with another woman.

Young Eddie Reed, Belle's son, was even a potential suspect. Supposedly, he had asked for permission to ride her favorite horse to a party. She said no, but Eddie rode off on the horse anyway. He may have killed his mother because she whipped him for mistreating the horse.

Most chroniclers of the Old West insist that it was Edgar Watson who killed the Bandit Queen. After his acquittal, Watson, who believed July's threats to harm him, left the area with his family and moved to Arkansas. From there, he traveled to a remote spot in Florida on the Gulf of Mexico. Supposedly, he could not stay out of trouble and was eventually involved in the murders of six men. Watson met his end in typical Old West tradition—gunned down by deputies of the law.

~ The End of an Era ~

Belle Starr was just two days shy of forty-one years old when she died. But even during her short, turbulent lifetime, much had changed, not only to the Old West, but to the entire country.

The year Belle was born (1848), Wisconsin became the thirty-first state. By the time she died (1889), the country had added another ten states. North Dakota, South Dakota, Montana, and Washington all joined the Union that year.

Railroads were first introduced into the United States in 1825 when John Stephens built a steam locomotive on his front lawn in Hoboken, New Jersey. Even before Belle became a fugitive from the law, railroads were a fairly common—if not always reliable—form of transportation. And on May 10, 1869, the country was linked by railroad tracks when the Union Pacific, running westward from Council Bluffs, Iowa, met the Central Pacific, running eastward from Sacramento, California, at Promontory, Utah.

Belle Starr was born into a nation of about 20 million people. There were some 60 million Americans when she died. Electricity was a new invention during her lifetime. Thomas A. Edison introduced his incandescent lamp in 1879, and its use spread quickly to factories and homes. But Belle Starr didn't know about radios, and had probably never heard of an automobile. Radio became a reality only after Italian physicist Guglielmo Marconi perfected a system in 1901 that transmitted Morse code over the Atlantic Ocean.

Automobiles were produced in Europe in the 1880s, and by the century's end there were fifty auto companies in the United States. But the auto didn't really become popular in America until Henry Ford produced an inexpensive Model T with his assembly-line style of production. Twentieth-century outlaws quickly caught on to the use of the Model T as a getaway car, although the early ones were probably not any more reliable than a horse! Americans didn't start paying income tax until 1913. This was lucky for Belle—imagine if she had had to explain where all her money had come from!

The Starr Saga

What happened to the other people in Belle Starr's life?

In ill health, old Tom Starr was released from his Illinois prison in 1888. He went home to Briartown where he lived quietly until his death two years later.

Jim July Starr left Youngers' Bend after Watson was acquitted. Since he had jumped bond on the horse stealing charge, he was now a fugitive from the law. For a while he joined an outlaw gang and then hid out in the Cherokee Nation. In January 1890, a sheriff's posse tracked him down and shot him. July died a few days later in a prison hospital.

Eddie's Story

James Edwin "Eddie" Reed had been a worry to his mother for some time before her death. He was seventeen and resentful when July moved into the household at Youngers' Bend. Not surprisingly, considering his background, Eddie got into various minor troubles, for which Belle physically whipped him with her riding crop. In 1888, he was charged with horse stealing.

Eddie claimed that it was his companion, a Creek Indian boy, who had stolen the horse. Maybe it was his youth, or maybe the judge just believed him. In any case, Eddie got off and returned to Youngers' Bend. But relations between mother and son were strained. When, in December 1888, Belle's son asked to borrow one of her fine horses to go to a Christmas dance, she refused. Eddie took the horse anyway and abused it. Belle was furious and beat him severely. He left home. Belle later learned he had moved in with the Rowe family some distance away. She never saw Eddie again. When she visited the Rowe's ranch house in February, some hours before her death, Eddie had already left to see a friend.

When Eddie's horse stealing case came up in July, he was sentenced to the Ohio State Penitentiary at Columbus for five years. Pardoned in 1893, he went to see his sister, Pearl, who was now running a house of prostitution. Back in the Cherokee Nation, he was arrested for smuggling whiskey in 1894, but the case was thrown out for lack of evidence.

Surprisingly enough, Eddie Reed turned his life around. He married, settled down, and became a deputy marshall. By all accounts, he was a good one. What would Belle have thought of her son being a lawman? In December 1896, while trying to arrest two men for selling whiskey, Eddie Reed was shot and killed. He was twenty-five years old.

Pearl's Story

After Belle's death, Pearl married Will Harrison, but the marriage ended in divorce in 1891. She began working in a brothel, saying she needed the money to secure a pardon for Eddie, who was then in prison. She did manage to hire attorneys who secured Eddie's release in 1893.

After that, Pearl started her own business in Fort Smith, where she met Eddie again after he was freed. He was so upset at what his sister was doing that he told her he wished he had stayed in prison. But Pearl ignored him. In 1894, she gave birth to a second daughter, named Ruth. (Her first daughter, Flossie, was given up for adoption.) Three years later, she married a musician named Arthur Erbach. They had a son, who soon died of malaria, as did Pearl's husband. A fourth child, Jennette, was born in 1902 to Pearl and Dell Andrews, a horse trader.

A few years later, Pearl put both daughters in a convent in St. Louis and began a slow slide in and out of jail for moral violations and possession of liquor. She died in Douglas, Arizona, on July 6, 1925. Her daughter buried her in the Calvary Cemetery under the name of Rosa Reed.

Belle Starr is buried at Youngers' Bend beneath a white marble gravestone. It bears the image of her favorite horse, Venus, as well as a bell to the left and a star to the right. Beneath are these words:

> *Belle Starr.*
> *Born in Carthage Mo.*
> *Feb 5, 1848.*
> *Died*
> *Feb 3, 1889.*
> *"Shed not for her the bitter tear,*
> *Nor give the heart to vain regret,*
> *'Tis but the casket that lies here,*
> *The gem that filled it sparkles yet."*

Chronology

The Life of Belle Starr

February 5, 1848	Myra Maybelle Shirley born in Jasper County, Missouri.
1856	Moves with family to Carthage, Missouri.
1862	Becomes a spy for the Confederacy.
June 1864	Brother Bud, a Confederate guerrilla fighter, is killed by Union troops; rest of family moves to Scyene, Texas.
November 1866	Marries Jim Reed.
September 1868	Daughter Pearl born; brother Edwin killed by Texan law officers.
1869	Moves to Los Angeles, California with Reed, who is wanted for murder.
February 1871	Son James Edwin Reed born.
August 1874	Reed is killed by lawmen.
June 1880	Marries Sam Starr and moves to Youngers' Bend in Cherokee Territory.
1880-1882	Supposedly leads outlaw gang, gains reputation as "Bandit Queen."
February 1883	Put on trial in Fort Smith, Arkansas, with Starr for horse stealing; sentenced to one year in prison.
1886	Sam Starr killed in fight with lawman; Jim July moves in with Belle at Youngers' Bend.
1887	July charged with horse stealing.
February 3, 1889	Shot and killed while riding home from a friend's, almost certainly by Edgar Watson, who was acquitted of the crime; buried at Youngers' Bend.

The Life of the Nation

1820	Missouri is admitted to the Union as a slave state under the Missouri Compromise.
1843	Missionary Marcus Whitman leads 1,000 settlers along the Oregon Trail to the northwest.
January 1948	Gold is discovered at Sutter's Mill, California, setting off the California Gold Rush.
1854	The Nebraska territory is divided into two states, Nebraska and Kansas, under the Kansas-Nebraska Act.
April 12, 1861	Confederate soldiers fire on Fort Sumter in South Carolina; the Civil War begins.
July 21, 1861	The First Battle at Bull Run (Manassas), Virginia, ends in a Southern victory.
July 1–3, 1862	Southern troops under General Robert E. Lee are defeated at the Battle of Gettysburg, Pennsylvania.
August 21, 1863	Quantrill's Raiders, Confederate guerrilla fighters, attack Lawrence, Kansas, and kill at least 150 people.
April 9, 1865	Lee surrenders to Union General Ulysses S. Grant at Appomattox Court House, effectively ending the Civil War.
February 13, 1866	The James gang commits the first daytime bank robbery in the United States in Liberty, Missouri.
May 10, 1869	The Union Pacific and Central Pacific Railroads meet at Promontory, Utah, completing the first transcontinental railroad.
1873	Samuel Colt invents his six-shot, side-action revolver, the "Peacemaker."
1876	Six of the James' gang are killed during a bank robbery in Northfield, Minnesota.
October 26, 1881	The Earp brothers and Doc Holliday meet the Clanton and McLaury brothers at the famous gunfight at the O.K. Corral in Tombstone, Arizona.
April 3, 1882	Jesse James is killed in his home in St. Joseph, Missouri, by a friend, Robert Ford.
1889	North Dakota, South Dakota, Montana, and Washington are admitted to the Union.

Glossary

Acquit   To find not guilty.

Armory   Storage place for weapons.

Autobiography   A book in which a person tells about his or her life.

Bail   An amount of money that is paid that allows a person freedom until a trial finds the person innocent or guilty.

Buckskins   Soft material made from the skin of deer or sheep.

Census   An official count of people living in a certain area.

Cholera   A very serious, or deadly, disease that attacks the intestines and causes severe diarrhea.

Compromise   To agree to something that combines two different points of view on an issue.

Confederate   Having to do with the Confederacy during the Civil War.

Exploits   Daring adventures.

Fugitive   A person who has run away from the law.

Gallows   A frame that was once used for hanging criminals

Guerrilla   A person who belongs to a small group of soldiers who attack the official forces.

Larceny   The taking of another person's property unlawfully.

Outpost   A remote frontier settlement.

Penitentiary   Jail.

Proprietor   Owner.

Quota   A set amount of something.

Shrouded   Covered or hidden.

Stereotype   An opinion of a person or idea that is overly simplified.

Tavern   A bar or an inn.

Source Notes

Chapter One

Page 8: "Now she dashed away through the narrow gulch…" Mary Noel. "Dime Novels." *American Heritage*, February 1956, p. 50.

Page 11: "Carthage Hotel, North Side Public Square…" Glenn Shirley. *Belle Starr and Her Times*. Norman, OK: Univ. of Oklahoma Press, 1982, p. 36.

Page 24: "I could see every house…" Geoffrey C. Ward. *The West: An Illustrated History*. Boston, MA: Little, Brown and Company, 1996. p. 54.

Chapter Two

Page 30: "Go West, young man, and grow up with the country." William A. Degregorio. *The Complete Book of U.S. Presidents*. New York: Barricade, 1993, p. 267.

Page 34: "October 1st saw us—a wagon…Time-Life Books (editors) *The Wild West*. New York, NY: Time-Life Books, 1993, p. 54.

Chapter Three

Page 54: "My eye was caught..." Ward, p. 120.

Page 55: "The blacksmith..." Duncan, p. 36.

Page 57: "Dear Brother Marion:…" Phillip W. Stelle. *Starr Tracks: Belle and Pearl Starr*. Gretna, LA: Pelican Publishing Company, 1989, pp. 41-42.

Chapter Four

Page 62: "…no part that could be recovered, my said husband having spent of disposed of all that he had and having left me in a destitute condition." Shirley, p. 128.

Chapter Five

Pages 67: "On the 5th day of June …" Shirley, pp. 140-141.

Page 78: "I have been estranged..." Ibid., p. 147.

Chapter Six

Page 81: "In the U.S. district court last week..." Shirley, p. 161.

Page 85: "The next time a lady..." Ibid., p. 171.

Page 98: "A Desperate Woman Killed." Ibid., p. 3.

Chapter Seven

Page 105: "Belle Starr Born in Carthage, Missouri…" Steele, p. 70.

Further Reading

Altman, Linda Jacobs. *The California Gold Rush in American History.* (In American History). Springfield, NJ: Enslow Publishers, Inc., 1997.

Green, Carl R., and Sanford, William R. *Calamity Jane: A Frontier Original* (Legendary Heroes of the Wild West). Springfield, NJ: Enslow Publishers, Inc., 1996.

Hamilton, John. *Jesse James* (Heroes & Villains of the Wild West). Minneapolis, MN: Abdo Publishing Company, 1996.

Krohn, Katherine E. *Women of the Wild West* (A&E Biography). Minneapolis, MN: Lerner Publications Company, 2000.

Marvis, B. *Belle Starr* (Legends of the West). New York, NY: Chelsea House, 2000.

Sandler, Martin W. *Civil War* (Library of Congress Books). New York, NY: HarperCollins Juvenile Books, 1996.

Savage, Jeff. *Cowboys and Cow Towns of the Wild West* (Trailblazers of the Wild West). Springfield, NJ: Enslow Publishers, Inc., 1995.

Savage, Jeff. *Pioneering Women of the Wild West* (Trailblazers of the Wild West). Springfield, NJ: Enslow Publishers, Inc., 1995.

Wukovits, John F. *Annie Oakley* (Legends of the West). New York, NY: Chelsea House, 1997.

Wukovits, John F. *Wyatt Earp* (Legends of the West). New York, NY: Chelsea House, 1997.

Web Sites

To find out more about the West, including Native Americans and cowboys, go to: **www.thewildwest.org**

For more information on the Trail of Tears, go to:**www.rosecity.net/tears**

To learn more about the California gold rush, go to: **www.pbs.org/goldrush**

For more information on the Oregon Trail and the nation's other historic routes, go to:
www.gorp.com/gorp/resource/us_trail/ore.htm

To learn about the Santa Fe Trail, go to: **www.nmhu.edu/research/sftrail**

To read more about the West, go to: **www.pbs.org/weta/thewest**

Index

BELLE STARR AND THE WILD WEST

Photo Credits